Flávia Gonçalves Fernandes

BUSINESS INFORMATION SYSTEMS

Flávia Gonçalves Fernandes

BUSINESS INFORMATION SYSTEMS

Governance and Business Intelligence

ScienciaScripts

Imprint

Cover image: www.ingimage.com

This book is a translation from the original published under ISBN 978-620-5-50660-8.

Publisher:
Sciencia Scripts
is a trademark of
Dodo Books Indian Ocean Ltd. and OmniScriptum S.R.L publishing group

120 High Road, East Finchley, London, N2 9ED, United Kingdom
Str. Armeneasca 28/1, office 1, Chisinau MD-2012, Republic of Moldova, Europe
Printed at: see last page
ISBN: 978-620-6-19736-2

SUMMARY

CHAPTER 1 2
CHAPTER 2 12
CHAPTER 3 19
CHAPTER 4 32

CHAPTER 1

ORGANIZATIONAL BEHAVIOR IN INFORMATION TECHNOLOGY

Abstract: This *paper aims as one of its objectives to present and conceptualize Information Technology (IT) and Organizational Behavior (OC), exposing their developments, their impacts and giving due importance to each of these factors within the organizational environment. For the creation of this article it was used bibliographical means and research via internet. We consider that the junction between IT and CO, when done in an efficient and effective manner only brings gains, competitive advantage, and other factors that will only contribute to the expansion of the organization.*

Keywords: *Organizational Behaviour, Information Technology, Organization.*

1. INTRODUCTION

Being Information Technology (IT) as an area of great importance within organizations, and the Organizational Behavior serving as a basis for studying the behavior of individuals, groups and structures in the business conviviality, we can state that the synergy between these two areas, when managed efficiently, can cause the growth, development, competitive advantage and a strategic improvement in the company's management. Given the above, the work aims to analyze the influence of information technology in various areas mainly in organizational behavior and how its management is performed.

1.1. What is information technology and organisational behaviour

With technology becoming increasingly present in our daily lives, whether through casual activities or even those that are routine, such as talking to a friend, sending a message, and even domestic activities, information technology has also found itself present in the daily routines of the vast majority of workers, in order to facilitate their work activities, giving more peace of mind and convenience to those who enjoy the benefits it provides.

In our day-to-day life we can see technology used in smartphones, cars, watches, computers, etc., aiming to improve the quality of life or facilitate our daily activities. In the business environment it is present in the machines used by large companies that end up replacing human hands, in software that facilitates the tasks of most employees, and in virtually most of the organizational environment, because Information Technology is an area that has been growing a lot over the years.

However, in a clearer way we can define IT as being an agglomeration of digital solutions that provide storage, registration and analysis of data that has been captured, and can, as previously stated, be applied in various branches of global, business or personal activities.

Within an organization, something that also helps and has a great impact on the success and development of the company is the organizational behavior, composed by values, goals, beliefs and culture of that corporation. And behaviour is defined as the variable that dictates the way in which people relate to each other. We can thus classify organisational behaviour as being the way in which individuals, in their organisational environment, live together, exchange experiences and treat each other.

In other words, it is people who manipulate and are responsible for the organisational climate, the unity of groups within companies, objectives, among other factors, since their success is the result of well-structured organisational behaviour.

1.2. Evolution of information technology in organisations

Previously, in the organisational environment, most of these companies used data processing only to control operational data, stock, payroll, among others.

As time went by, information technology began to establish itself and innovated the way in which companies use technological means, bringing integration between all the existing systems in the organisation.

The evolution of Information Technology (IT) can be divided into four periods, with the first period starting in the 1960s, when computers became important pieces for corporations, with emphasis on improvements in hardware, speed, etc.

The second period started around 1970 and was more focused on improvements in computer software and its adaptation to the needs of each corporation, resulting in increasingly efficient data processing systems.

The third period was marked by innovations that brought ease and practicality in the day-to-day lives of those who used technological means to work, the creation of the Help Desk (a consultation network, in which users could clarify pending issues and receive advice in the technological area) was of great help.

It was only in the 1990's that computers and microcomputers finally became compatible, facilitating the access and exchange of information within companies. It was during this period that IT developed and came to carry the burden of being a tool of global importance and of indispensable use for any type of process that takes place within companies.

1.3. Organisational Behaviour towards IT

We can define O.C. as the study of the behaviour of individuals within an organisation, with the viral purpose of applying this knowledge to improve the effectiveness of a company. To contribute to this study we have some disciplines that are used in the same line of reasoning as sociology, psychology, social psychology, anthropology and political science. This study seeks conclusions of behavior with proven scientific evidence, because many times we analyze profiles according to our intuition and not the veracity of the facts.

The organization needs to increase its income and this idea has been around for a long time. With this in mind, the Administration seeks solutions so that within the organization there are fewer conflicts and maximum performance, always seeking improvements for the organizational institution.

Within these improvements we highlight the importance of Information Technology, with globalization has become possible new changes and technology is of great value, but you need to plan before using it, choose a reliable system, understand how it works then not to cause greater costs and a tool so useful needs to be understood and valued, Because the benefits are immense and brings many advantages, such as reducing the costs of operations, get higher productivity numbers which generates a positive basis for competition, use of systems where you can view all kinds of reports, making decisions are taken quickly and reliably, making the service more organized, structured.

Technology is a function often used in organizations and in some places as something common, not having dimension of how to add and make it for itself an advantage over the competition, because many do not understand how far technology can reach and how it can be beneficial using as a strategic tool, a company can transform itself, the interest and knowledge by technology makes a big difference in the performance of the organization.

With the correct use of Information Technology, it can be understood that performance, agility and practicality are real and strongly contribute to the increase of competitiveness in organisations, making use of social networks, where millions of people can get to know the company, its vision, values and history.

Simply put, IT in itself has become and still is an exceptional ally for companies to achieve their goals by displaying their product to society in a fast and practical way.

However, it is still common for some organizations to spend millions on technology and unfortunately not get a pleasant return, because there are many IT services provided in a totally wrong way, causing the organization to lose money and often even customers. This function needs to be aligned with the goals of the organization so that this important tool can provide a beneficial result, where value will be added to the business as a whole.

Information technology, as said before, is very beneficial, but it needs to be planned and studied, and the organisation needs to know how to use IT to its advantage considering an internal and external analysis of the environment itself, in this way it will be possible to achieve the established objectives of each collaborator.

1.4. Technology-intensive organisation

Organisations are present on the market for presenting a product, an idea, a service provision with a view to profit and organisational growth. However, the organisational world is not static, it is constantly changing, whether externally or internally.

And for companies to continue exercising their activities they must be willing to change, since time is no longer the same, it has shortened, communications, businesses to be solved between departments, productions can no longer be rigid and slow. It is time for an organisation with flexibility, speed, permeable frontiers which enable a more agile reaction to the changes taking place in the environment, and these organisations are the so-called E-Organisations.

According to Nilson, Pasternak and Viscio (2000), E-Organizations are the organizations formed of intense information technology, which changes the way of doing business, the organizational actors are repositioned and finally the organization is transformed, the E-Organizations have models of adaptable and dynamic operations, and its operation does not suffer from interruption, which allows to act quickly and efficiently. Moreover, the use of technology is enabling a better and more effective relationship with customers, suppliers and even more creating a network in which knowledge is shared among employees through information systems, in addition to empowering people even more.

1.5. Strategic role of IT in organisations

The term "Information Technology" serves to designate the set of technological and computational resources for the generation and use of information

(Rezende, 200). IT is used to disseminate improvements in internal processes, reduce costs, apply better control, add value to services and products offered by the organization among others. In view of its purpose, today, IT plays an important role in organizational planning, in decision making and in the company's strategy.

The main function of IT is to make information result in a strategic plan that defines the future direction of resources, reflecting the policies, standards and procedures of information resources as a whole, thus providing support to the sectors of the organization. The plan is the matrix point for any investment in technology, identifying future changes that should be included in the organization's plans.

As shown, IT has an importance in organizational planning and organizational processes as a whole. The need to think strategically comes since the industrial revolution in which the value of this administrative process was seen.

Thus the IT domain is acquiring a status as a development and strategy definition agent at different levels. Henderson & Venkatraman (1993) proposed a model that highlights and analyses the strategic importance of the role played by IT within companies. The proposed model is based on internal and external corporate factors. An analysis is conducted of the IT impact on the company's business, how this affects the organization and the IT strategy and also what is available on the market in terms of new technologies. The proposal presented is called "Strategic Alignment Model".

Tabela 3 – Características das Perspectivas de Alinhamento Estratégico

PERSPECTIVA	IMPULSIONADORA	PAPEL DA ALTA DIREÇÃO DA EMPRESA	PAPEL DA DIREÇÃO DE TI	CRITÉRIO DE DESEMPENHO
1 EXECUÇÃO DA ESTRATÉGIA	ESTRATÉGIA DE NEGÓCIOS	FORMULADOR DE ESTRATÉGIAS	IMPLANTADOR DE ESTRATÉGIAS	CUSTOS/CENTROS DE SERVIÇO
2 TRANSFORMAÇÃO TECNOLÓGICA	ESTRATÉGIA DE NEGÓCIOS	FORNECEDOR DE VISÃO DE TECNOLOGIA	ARQUITETO DE TECNOLOGIA	LIDERANÇA TECNOLÓGICA
3 POTENCIAL COMPETITIVO	ESTRATÉGIA DE TI	VISIONÁRIO DE NEGÓCIOS	CATALISADOR	LIDERANÇA DE NEGÓCIOS
4 NÍVEL DE SERVIÇO	ESTRATÉGIA DE TI	PRIORIZADOR	LIDERANÇA EXECUTIVA	SATISFAÇÃO DO CLIENTE

(Adaptado de HENDERSON & VENKATRAMAN, 1993)

The first premise of the Strategic Alignment Model is that external and internal factors must be considered in this planning. The second is that effective management with the use of IT requires a balance between decisions in all sectors of the company. This model highlights the importance of information technology and its processes help the manager in reallocating resources, improving projects, decision making, structure and the organizational set.

1.6. Internet and Social Media as an influence on Organizational Behaviour

The digital era is constantly evolving, this makes organizations strive to keep up with the speed of this evolution. These changes generate constant impacts on society and on people's lives, anticipating more and more the changes in the market that becomes more dynamic and competitive (CHIAVENATO, 2011). The social networks correspond to a structural system of influence in organizations with potential for involvement of people and institutions in a participatory, dynamic and democratic way, arising from common purposes, values and objectives (OLIVIERI, 2003). Based on these assumptions of Chiavenato and Olivieri, technology comes into play to form group of personal interaction and exchange of information and knowledge for organizations.

Communicating has always been one of the needs of the human being, and with the advent of the internet that provides a type of interaction. The dilemma is that this interaction used in the organization is not always used for professional purposes, which is why organizations end up blocking access to social networking sites, because people use for other purposes which ends up compromising the performance in their activities.

This interaction with Technology and organizational behavior brings its advantages and disadvantages. Bringing out the advantages, the speed of the expansion of people integrated into these channels is influencing companies in the market, selling their products and services. According to the 2009 IEL Magazine, social networks are also fundamental in collecting information from consumers, offer real time communication, allow the company to connect with the professional world, and etc. Thus, the use of the internet and social networks in the departments does not only have disadvantages, but also allows the company to know its people and its market, strengths and weaknesses and helps in the optimization and development.

Starting from the prism that it is indispensable for any process, relations and structure of the organization, the adoption of specific means and its management form may be adequate or inadequate. The disadvantages are: the use of this technology may expose restricted company data, use of digital networks for personal use, employee dispersion and unreliable surfing and virus-infested sites. With this new context, organizations started to exchange information in a minimum time in which information technology caused the emergence of the globalization of the economy.

The competitiveness has become more intense among organizations, having them to adapt, having better agility, innovation and making necessary changes to support the new threats and opportunities in the current market (SCHEIN, 2010).

The communication and the evolution of technology, brought the need for information systems and social networks as an important role in corporate communication, getting faster and closer to the customer. However, the use of social networks ends up being practiced in a beneficial way for the development of this tool and behavior of the organization, because many employees access the social networks during the working day, since some people use it for professional means, but there are those who use it for personal means.

1.7 How IT in conjunction with Organisational Behaviour contribute to the growth of the organisation

Technology has a major impact on organisational structure, influencing culture, policies and management modes.

The organisational structures of a company are the users and the generators of information. Having a well organised structure, with defined departments, formality of processes and a harmonious relationship among all, favours the performance of the Information Systems.

Therefore, it is very important that managers establish a relationship between IT and all the company's departments, individuals and groups, engaging them in a strategic manner in order to help bring positive results to the organisation, leading it, finally, to organisational growth.

2. METHODOLOGY

In order to make this work possible, bibliographical research was used, through reliable websites and literary works that deal with the subject.

3. CONCLUDING REMARKS

Given the above, we must consider and give due importance to the IT area of any organization, whether large, medium or small, taking and bringing information, processing data and delivering them in a fast and practical way to those who need it, being responsible for integration and sharing between all systems of the company, and for being an area that evolves overtime and is now at its peak, being essential for the growth and development of any enterprise.

Therefore, if there is good management in organisational behaviour, that is, when people are aware of their actions within the company, when they know how the organisational processes work and their whys, among other factors, organisational development will be an easily reachable factor.

REFERENCES:

THE EVOLUTION OF IT TO THE PRESENT DAY. Available at < https://www.portaleducacao.com.br/conteudo/artigo s/farmacia/a-evolucao-do-ti-ate-the-current-days/56111> Accessed 12 Aug 18

THE IMPORTANCE OF IT FOR SUCCESS THE COMPANY. Available at <blog.loupen.com.br/a-importance-of-ti-for-the-success-of-the-business/> Accessed 12 Aug. 2018

ANDRADE, Antonio Rodrigues de, ORGANISATIONS' BEHAVIOR AND STRATEGIES IN TIMES OF CHANGE

GOVERNANCE OF INFORMATION TECHNOLOGY INFORMATION. Available at < https://www.devmedia.com.br/governanca-de-tecnologia-da-informacao/13826> Accessed 12 Aug. 2018

LAURINDO, Fernando José Barbin; SHIMIZU, Tamio; CARVALHO, Marly Monteiro de; JUNIOR, Roque Rabechini. MANAGEMENT AND PRODUCTION: THE ROLE OF INFORMATION TECHNOLOGY (TI) IN THE STRATEGY OF ORGANIZATIONS. Pág. 160 à 179, 2001.

THE NEW PROFILE OF ORGANISATIONAL BEHAVIOUR IN COMPANIES IT DAILY. Available at <https://www.classecontabil.com.br/o-novo-perfil- of-organisational-behaviour-in-companies-before-ti/> Accessed 12 Aug. 2018

TECNOLOGIA DA INFORMAÇÃO APLICADA A SISTEMAS DE INFORMAÇÃO EMPRESARIAIS: O PAPEL ESTRATÉGICO DA INFORMAÇÃO E DOS SISTEMAS DE INFORMAÇÃO NAS EMPRESAS. 9ª ed. São Paulo: Atlas, 2013. Authors: Denis Alcides Rezende. Aline França de Abreu

CHAPTER 2

INFORMATION SYSTEMS

Abstract: *This project aims to define what is information system, how they can act in organizations, in order to answer the following research guiding question: How can the information system be in my cycle in the organization? To this end, it will be carried out a qualitative research of exploratory type to be able to answer the questions about the theme. The collected data will be analyzed from the creation of axes and categories of analysis defined from the material obtained in the field research. At the end of this work, it is expected to have a more malleable knowledge on the subject and also understand its importance in our daily lives.*

Keywords: *Information System. Information management. Technology*.

INFORMATION SYSTEMS

WHAT ARE INFORMATION SYSTEMS?

Information Systems bring together a collection of data collected through software created by programmers and that in the future will be used for an organisation's decision-making process. For data to be collected it must have a purpose. An example is the data collection of the students of a school, that when collecting the students' data to enroll them, it can help in the issuance of school reports or in the monitoring of the students' productivity afterwards. Another case would be in an Academy, it is common that they do before the enrolment of their customers the collection of some data, such as CPF, a frontal photo, date of birth, etc.. And that later will facilitate its management. And for an information system to exist it is necessary to have a person that uses the data.

INFORMATION TECHNOLOGY + DATA + PROCEDURE + PEOPLE

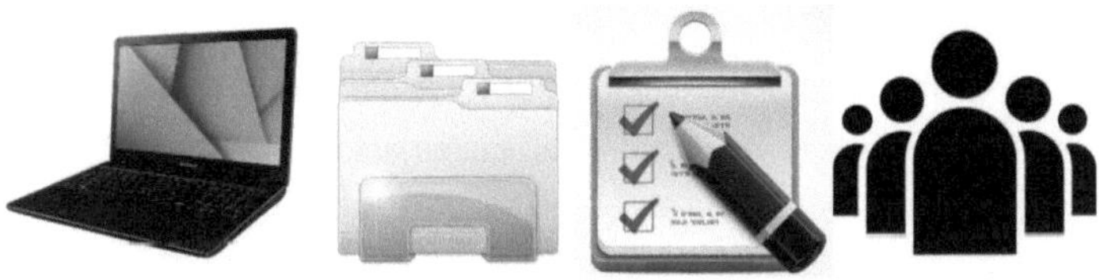

Figure 1. Information Systems encompass information technology, data, data processing procedures and people who use the data (Gordon, Judith R./2006)

WHAT IS THE IMPORTANCE OF INFORMATION SYSTEMS?

With the evolution of technology resulting from the 4th industrial revolution and the increase of competitiveness among companies, information systems are created as an aid in the decision making process, the minimization of costs and flexibility of communication .

Today the companies have software that helps in the purchase of raw materials, searching for the best price among several suppliers, helps in the communication between the collaborators of a company, in a more practical way, creates production and quality forms. And they help in the proximity between client and company.

INFORMATION SYSTEMS AS A SUPPORT FOR INFORMATION MANAGEMENT

There are three categories of information systems: automation system, transaction processing system and management support system. All three help in information management. The automation system, as the name implies, is used to automate processes in order to facilitate them, reduce costs, etc. This type of system can be implemented in several ways by a manager, such as the use of barcode readers in supermarkets, to facilitate and speed up customer service.

And the collection of information by this automated system will become what we call the Transaction Processing System (TPS), the use of the bar code reader has the function of controlling the output of products, through this control the manager can ask several questions: 1º When did I sell a certain product this month? 2º What was the total value of sales for a certain period?

The management support systems (MSSs) assist in the activities of managers, this type of system provides important information to a manager as a way to support decision making.

The manager before implementing any system should first ask if this system meets their demands and that before its implementation train their employees to operate, a poor planning can affect the company.

DIFFERENCES BETWEEN VERTICAL X HORIZONTAL SOFTWARE

In IT we have vertical and horizontal software, each of these two types of software has certain characteristics:

VERTICAL SOFTWARE	HORIZONTAL SOFTWARE
Common in a certain type of company	They are common in many companies/industries
They are developed separately to meet the needs of a company	They are developed to serve a mass
Example: Line and Railway Software	
Greater Cost Benefit	Lowest cost benefit
Acquired in small quantities	Purchased in larger quantities

Many companies at the beginning of their career tend to buy less specialized (horizontal) software to meet their routine information needs. As they grow and the need for more specific information arises, they will need more specialised software.

It is necessary at the time of choosing software to choose that which best suits the needs of the company and has the best cost-benefit.

WEBSITES AS A WAY OF INTERMEDIATING THE RELATIONSHIP WITH SUPPLIERS

To improve logistics, Garrett Engine Boosting Systems Division of Honeywell International has created a website where all its suppliers have access to the stock amounts of certain products, so they can know if a particular product needs replacement without having to contact Honeywell International in person.

ACCOUNTING SYSTEMS IN DECISION MAKING

The Accounting systems are the most common in companies, they manage accounts payable and receivable, elaborate ratios for all the company's accounts, do the automatic depreciation accounting of fixed assets, etc.

MANAGEMENT TECHNOLOGIES THAT COMPANIES SHOULD EMBRACE

Cloud and SaaS

The term Cloud means the provision of software solutions via the Internet on a shared infrastructure of servers and other equipment.

Big Data

Big Data is the term used to describe a large or complex amount of information that traditional applications to analyse it are not sufficient. Organisations generate more and more information, as they are becoming more computerised every day.

Systems record user interaction information such as:

- Access logs
- Operations
- History

Mooc

MOOCs, an acronym for Massive Open Online Courses, are courses offered over the internet for free and usually with many enrollees.

Gamification

Gamification is the name given to experiences similar to games. It consists of contextualising an activity or a set of activities in an environment similar to a game, with rules, objectives, phases and awards.

Gamification is not exactly a technology, but an experience that can be implemented by people management using technology or not. Today several solutions aimed at HR use this technique in its dynamic use.

- The completion of a course
- The achievement of a goal
- The sharing of content

IoT - Internet of Things

Internet of Things. The term serves to describe the communication network between devices that are connected to the internet. Such as *smartphones*, *smartwatches*, cars, buildings, etc.

Mobile

This is one of the most obvious technologies that is already in widespread use. In Brazil, the number of smartphones reached 168 million in 2016 according to the

Annual Survey of Administration and Use of Information Technology in Companies conducted by FGV-SP and the trend is increasing.

- Spreading its culture
- Keep it up to date
- Allow access to information

Social Networks and Videos

Video is undoubtedly one of the most engaging types of content. This type of media had a more complicated and costly production in the past, but today everyone who owns a smartphone can produce, edit them easily and share.

In the world of work, this practice is still little encouraged, but it can have many impacts on the employee's daily life.

Allied to corporate social networks, which are becoming increasingly common, the production of video content and its sharing in the workplace is an excellent strategy for dissemination, retention and knowledge management in the organisation.

THE ADVANTAGES THAT A MANAGEMENT SYSTEM CAN OFFER YOUR COMPANY

- The management system integrates all areas of the company ;
- Consolidated view of the various sales channels ;
- Optimisation of the use of working capital;
- Reduction of rework ;
- Strategic management of people;
- Decision-making support;
- Reduced costs increased profits;
- Abolition of various software;
- Reduction of errors;
- Reduction of losses.

INTEGRATED BUSINESS MANAGEMENT SYSTEM

A management system is a computer program developed to assist in the management of business. They are used in all sectors of the company, regardless of the size and the branch of activity of the business. They are also known as ERP - *Enterprise Resource Planning.*

CONCLUDING REMARKS

The work made an analysis of how the technology has been more useful for the society. The information management is important in our common environment, where, we had a focus that all aspects related to IS and IT provides us with tools that help us a lot for agility in processes, decision making in the organization, new knowledge bases, among others.

REFERENCES

https://www.foccoerp.com.br/gestao-de-empresas/sistema-de-gestao-integrada/ >accessed on 24/08/18

https://impulse.net.br/tecnologias-gestao-de-pessoas/ > accessed 23/08/18

https://www.erpflex.com.br/blog/7-vantagens-de-um-sistema-de-gestao > accessed 26/08/18

GORDON, STEVEN R. / GORDON, JUDITH R. **Information System**: A Managerial Approach. LTC 2006. Rio de Janeiro.

CHAPTER 3

INFORMATION TECHNOLOGY GOVERNANCE

Abstract: *Information technology has assumed an important role in the ways of managing organizations, since it is able to assist in the decision-making process regarding internal and external issues, for this reason, investments in the IT area grow substantially, and companies seek to adopt Governance of Information Technology initiatives, seeking to integrate and align IT to the business objectives in order to add value to the company and achieve the competitive advantage needed to stay in the market. The objective of this article is to present general concepts of Governance of Information Technology, its main aspects and discuss its contribution to support the strategic management of information. To this end, the theories of the main authors of the literature on the subject were analyzed, as well as scientific articles related to the theme that attest its relevance for organizations.*

Keywords: *Information Technology. IT Governance. Corporate Governance. Management.*

1. INTRODUCTION

Organizations today face a highly competitive scenario in a fully globalized world, while new business models emerge at a fast pace and others cease to exist, new products and services are launched every day and the consumer assumes an even more demanding posture. Thus, companies are in constant search for strategies to anticipate the tastes and needs of the market and remain competitive, at this point, information technology can be a powerful ally to achieve competitive advantage.

The GTI (Governance of Information Technology) is associated with Corporate Governance, a theme that only gained prominence in administrative research after corporate scandals with manipulation of accounting data in the 2000s, such as the Enron case in the United States and later in the 2008 real estate crisis. The absence of financial transparency in organizations was the cause of incalculable losses both for organizations and for countries and societies affected by economic stagnation.

For this reason, organisations have begun to demand a set of governance mechanisms aimed at transparency and security for shareholders and investors. The American law "The

U.S. Public Company Accounting Reform and Investor Protection Act of 2002", the Sarbane-Oxley (SOX), related to corporate governance and business ethics in companies with capital on the New York Stock Exchange, although in force only in the USA, was an incentive to extend the adoption of the concept of corporate governance in the area of information technology (Miorando and Ribeiro, 2014).

It is important to emphasize that Corporate Governance has its bases formed on control and responsibility, however, it also considers the decision structures and articulation among the sectors of the organization; values also adopted by the GTI, which has methods to make more transparent, organized and legitimate the practices of direction and monitoring of the company's performance.

Organizations are concerned about protecting their *stakeholders*. Investments in Corporate Governance reflect on the company's value. Presenting good Governance makes investors agree to pay more for the shares, since it will be a reliable organization.

When an organisation brings trust to the market there is consequently an improvement in the company's economy, not necessarily related to the production and sale of products or services, but on the ability to preserve the functioning of processes satisfactorily and to grant value to *stakeholders*.

2. CORPORATE GOVERNANCE

Normally the use of the term governance in the administrative scope, composing the strategic planning of the organization, according to the Guide of the Brazilian Institute of Corporate Governance (IBGC) can be defined as "the system through which the organizations are directed, monitored and encouraged, involving the relationship between the Council, the executive team and other control bodies. Good governance practices convert principles into objective recommendations, aligning interests with the purpose of preserving the organisation's reputation and optimising its social value, facilitating its access to resources and contributing to its longevity".

Corporate Governance stipulates a set of actions, rules, customs, management and philosophy, which regulate the direction and management of the company and its link with the participants that compose it, which are the *stakeholders*. Among the purposes of Governance is to raise equity, equality and justice among its members, however, in publicly traded organizations, shareholders, board, and executives are the most influential *stakeholders.*

3. IT GOVERNANCE

IT governance is the expression used to portray the way the people in charge of the governance of a company will apply IT in the supervision, monitoring, control and direction in the organization. The way IT will be effected will cause a great effect in relation to the achievement of the vision, mission and the strategic objectives of the organization (ITGI, 2003).

According to Weill and Ross (2006, p.8), ITM is "the specification of the decision-making rights and responsibilities framework to encourage desirable behaviours in the use of IT".

According to Professor João Roberto Peres: "IT Governance is a set of practices, standards and structured relationships, assumed by executives, managers, technicians and IT users of an organization, in order to ensure effective controls, expand security processes, minimize risks, increase performance, optimize the application of resources, reduce costs, support better decisions and consequently align IT to business.

Therefore, it is understood that organizations that intend to expand their demand for increased quality of their products and processes, which are concerned about standing out from the high competitiveness of the globalized market and seek to maximize their profits through lower costs and higher profits is interesting to have knowledge about IT Governance.

According Gotardo (2015) "IT Governance has as its main objective to store, process and make available information with quality and security, meeting the triad Confidentiality, Integrity and Availability (CID)".

Also according to the mentioned author, the implementation of governance should be combined with strategic management and with the roles and responsibilities of each group well defined. The definition of roles relates the leaders for decision making, and the delimitations of the mechanisms that will be structured.

According to ITGI (Information Technology Governance Institute), IT Management should be considered a duty of the executives and the board of directors, since they constitute the corporate governance that make up the leadership of the organization, being responsible for the formation of the organizational structure and the processes that ensure that IT will support and maintain the organizational strategies and goals.

A good example is Meg McCarthy, a member of the executive committee of Aetna, an American health insurance company says that "the organisation's IT is crucial to enabling the implementation of our business strategy. I report to the president of our company and am a member of the executive committee. In this capacity, I participate in all key business meetings and decisions that impact company strategy and technology strategy." (Reynolds, Stair, 2012).

It is essential that the IT area is aligned with the objectives and values of the organisation, that its efforts are focused on actions that add value to the business, that it is flexible to accommodate frequent changes, anticipate information and evaluate trends.

According to Edson Roberto Gaseta (2012) "(...)Such structures and processes seek to ensure that IT contributes so that the organization objectives and strategies assume their maximum value, in order to control the execution and the quality of IT services for the benefit of the organization. Basically, having a relationship structure and processes is to ensure that the actions of IT Governance are shared with the leaders of the organization (public or private), establishing the necessary processes to support the use of IT in the daily activities of users and customers, which form the internal and external public."

Peterson (2004) mentions that there is concern as to the relationship between investments and technologies and how they have been managed. Such facts have caused technology and business executives to acknowledge that the success of IT, currently, does not lie in the technology itself, but rather in how it is governed.

Research conducted by Jaeger Neto, Becker, Luciano and Testa in 2009 and Tarouco and Graeml in 2001 were crucial for the recognition of the importance of IT Management in the administration of companies in the country. The cited researchers indicated four variables-key to ITM that must be considered in the diagnoses of organizations in the country, they are: "Organizational structure and participation of IT and other areas in decision making about ITM; Business and IT alignment; Size and type of company; Relations between people and areas to understand the power relations and the flow of information.

However, despite being a significant issue on the agenda of organizations, the importance of the IT Management in the business success measures often does not maintain the level of relevance that should be attributed to it (Jaeger Neto *et al.*, 2009). Usually the ITM decisions are concentrated and are found in IT areas or business units, usually being linked to internal issues of the organization, i.e., the IT directions are related to cost reduction, instead of collaborating to innovative methods of doing business (Alves *et al.*, 2013).

Numerous studies show that the ITM is applied in organizations through a set of mechanisms related to the structure, the processes and the IT relationships aggregated with the various business areas (Peterson, 2004). The structures are correlated to the responsible for the IT actions and to those in charge of making decisions.

The processes are linked to the strategic direction and its monitoring by IT. In relationships are aggregated the participation of IT in other areas, the strategic dialogue, learning and appropriate communication (Van Grembergen, De Haes & Guldentops, 2004).

According to Van Grembergen *et al.*(2004), the procedures usually related to the IT decision-making structure are the delimitations of responsibilities and roles in IT, the IT structure in the company, the attendance of the CIO in the board of directors and the existence of a project office.

The ITM mechanisms related to processes are responsible for making IT managers and business areas work together so that the decision-making of both areas meet each other, executing and monitoring the application of decisions in a process of knowledge feedback of these projects (Ribbers, Peterson & Parker, 2002).

According to De Haes and Van Grembergen (2005) for the implementation of ITM it is necessary that the organization knows the *frameworks*, specific organizational models, available, with views to ensuring the success of ITM in their organization. The main *frameworks* are: the BSC, PMBok, CobiT, ITIL, CMMI and ISO 17.799.

The union between IT and the other business areas enables the solutions to problems or initiatives to have outputs congregated to the concrete needs of the business, transcending the functional boundaries (Lunardi, 2008). The mechanisms that perform this are the communication channels between the business and IT areas, thus it is possible to prepare an association plan that brings business needs closer to IT solutions and limitations (De Haes & Van Grembergen, 2005).

According to Lunardi (2008) situations may occur in which the IT processes and structure are harmonious, however, even so, due to relationship problems between IT and the business, it occurs a malfunction in the IT area. Therefore, the fundamental relationships mechanisms for governance, taking into account that communication is of utmost importance for the organization satisfactory operation, therefore, the better the communication about the governance mechanisms in the organization, the better its result will be.

Another important point is the learning sharing, which ensures the knowledge distribution between the business and IT areas so that IT remains combined to the organization purposes (Callahan & Keyes, 2004; De Haes & Van Grembergen, 2005). It is also worth remembering that sharing and knowledge management are simplified by some tools such as functional training between IT and areas, continuing education and the use of project banks (Lunardi, 2008).

3.1 Focus of IT Governance

Lunardi, Becker and Maçada (2010), highlight some areas as the essence of IT governance performance in organizations, they are: a) Strategic alignment - responsible for making the work done by IT and its priorities respond to the strategic needs agreed by the organization's business areas (ITGI, 2003); b) IT value - seeks to provide that IT applies to the business the intended benefits, within the deadlines and costs of the proposed investments; c) Risk management - related to the IT assets protection, both physical assets and information or services availability; d) IT resources - seeks to make the best use of the infrastructure and the IT knowledge of the organization, through investments and appropriate distribution of resources, whether with staff, data, support, technology, etc. (Lunardi, 2008); e) IT performance measurement - allow the follow-up and monitoring of the strategy implementation, processes, management and IT projects, in order to improve the IT value delivery to business; f) *Accountability* - aims to define for each IT decision who are the leaders and the various parties involved, and provide that the organization understands these structures. According to Van Grembergen *et al.* (2004) "it is a key point for good ITM".

GTI can be defined as "the management of management", because its fundamental function is to support the CIO (*Chief Information Officer*) in decision making so that the objectives of the organization are achieved, where the success of the implementation of the governance program will bring triumph to the organization, however, mistakes will probably bring failure to the company.

It is worth remembering that a governance programme can be ideal for one organisation and disastrous for another, requiring its own programme, since each organisation has its own particularities and needs.

Weill and Ross (2005) conducted a study of 300 companies around the world and did not identify an ideal formula for IT Governance, but concluded that high performing companies carefully design governance, managers in all companies make daily decisions putting the design into practice.

3.2 IT Governance Cycle

The IT Governance Cycle consists of four stages:

"1. Strategic Alignment and Compliance is about IT strategic planning being aligned with the organization's strategies considering its products and business segment, complying with legal and regulatory norms, the established policies and guidelines, avoiding any deviation or non-conformity.

2. Decision, Commitment, Prioritisation and Resource Allocation deals with the responsibilities for decisions involving IT, accounting for who, what, how and where decisions will be made, and concerns investments, application needs, IT architecture, infrastructure services, etc.

3. Structure, Processes, Operations and Management deals with the organizational and functional IT structure. It aligns systems operations, infrastructure, technical support, information security, management processes and the operation of IT products and services.

4. Performance Measurement deals with the selection, collection, and generation of the outcome indicators of IT processes, products and services and their impact on business strategies and objectives." (Gotardo, 2015).

The IT Governance cycle can be visualized as shown in figure 1 below: (FERNANDES and ABREU, 2008).

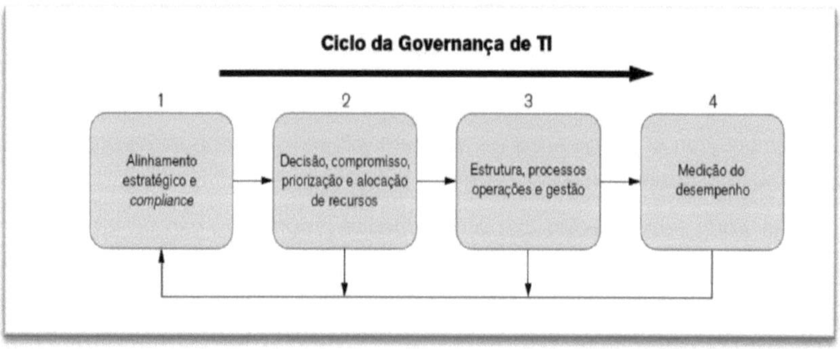

SOURCE: Estácio Web Aula Material

4. IT GOVERNANCE IN PUBLIC ADMINISTRATION

ITM is also relevant to the public sector, although there is no pretense of profit, the Public Administration bodies perform highly complex services, and with huge volumes of data, an inefficient IT sector is capable of delaying services and hinder processes, thus, it is essential that IT has adequate resources and is well managed.

Cunha and Souza Neto (2014) point out that "at a time when IT has become an indispensable factor to enable governments to offer better services to its citizens, in a more ethical, transparent, efficient and sustainable way, from an economic, environmental and social perspective, it has that the ITM emerges as a critical capacity for the public sector and its leaders, in search of creating and delivering more value to its citizens through the effective use of IT".

4.1 ITIL

Within the Federal Public Administration, there are guidelines on the ITM deployment, such as the Normative Instruction No. 4, of the Secretariat of Logistics and Information Technology, which provides on the IT services contracting in public agencies. The PDTI - Information Technology Master Plan used to direct the IT actions in the Public Administration bodies has a reference model to assist in its preparation, aiming to improve the IT management (GASETA, 2012).

5. FRAMEWORKS

Framework is a model with several functions that can be used by the developer, a good comparison is the toolbox, but instead of screwdrivers and hammers, there are bases for login forms, field validation and database connection. In this sense, as part of the trend to reduce costs and increase productivity, the use of this feature has become increasingly popular.

Today there is a huge variety of solutions available for the most diverse languages, with the possibility of testing and creating different functions according to the needs of each company. In order to be able to customise, it is necessary to use the principles of object orientation, such as abstraction, polymorphism and inheritance.

There are several benefits in the implementation of a *framework* and one of the main ones is the reduction of time in *software* development. Other reasons to use it in development projects are the reduction of *bugs*, ease of learning, code standardization and cost reduction.

Although the advantages of using a *framework* are greater than the disadvantages, it is worth pointing out that some practices should be observed and avoided, such as dependency, the complexity of modifying the *framework* and unnecessary code that can make the programme heavy.

Two *framework* models are widely used by managers in the definition of corporate strategy and objectives, being the Information Technology Infrastructure Library (ITIL) and the Control Objectives for Information and Related Technology (Cobit).

Although conceived as a recommendation guide for IT and telecom companies in the UK in the 1980s, it is still used today as a reference for a set of best practices for IT *service* management operations (such as *service desk*, incident, change, capacity, service level and security management) and for departmental alignment with the company's business. The focus is on the customer and on quality.

If implemented correctly, after a feasibility study, ITIL directly benefits IT governance and the way the area relates to the rest of the organization. It also brings other benefits, such as the reduction of task execution time and problem solving, increased user and customer satisfaction, greater management control and reduced operating costs.

It cannot be considered as a tool or solution, but rather as a flexible structure that can be adapted to the company's project management needs, but without losing sight of the quality of the services offered.

5.1 COBIT

COBIT was launched by ICASA in 1996, initially a set of control objectives that assisted in the audit of processes, practices and IT controls in the company. Thus, it focuses on the definition, implementation, supervision, measurement and improvement of process controls of the IT life cycle.

As defined by Gaseta (2012), "the COBIT is a set of information used as a reference model for IT Governance. It includes an executive summary, a *framework*, objectives control, audit maps, tools for implementation and a guide with management techniques. In addition, the COBIT is oriented to processes and business, based on controls and performance measures of IT processes".

In other words, COBIT helps prioritize and organize IT sector activities to meet corporate requirements. The *framework* allows for the identification of which processes have weak points and can negatively influence the department. Then, the management of these processes is prioritized.

5.2 ITIL *versus* COBIT

ITIL and COBIT are quite different from each other. Cobit has more affinity with process and control auditing, and ITIL is closer to IT service management.

While COBIT is primarily concerned with guiding organisations in implementing, operating and improving IT governance and management processes, ITIL offers best practice guidance for managing and executing IT services from the perspective of generating value to the business. More simply put, COBIT says 'what' and ITIL explains 'how'.

The two are like guides in the market, since they complement rather than compete. In the company, both should serve as reference, and not necessarily use all their aspects, since not all practices apply to the company.

This joint approach helps to solve problems and maximise the achievement of corporate goals, intensifying their strengths and adapting their use to the need. After all, implementation is not enough, you need continuous improvement in all processes and operations.

Together they form a strong foundation for IT governance and service management, regardless of whether they are internal, outsourced or business partner activities. Practitioners will have more options if they consider using the two models together.

6. CONCLUSION

It is undeniable that the constant technological transformations have substantially changed the business world. Specifically regarding information technology, so many possibilities have their advantages, such as the speed of communication and the ease of obtaining and storing data, however, one must be aware of the disadvantages, since the same technology if misused can be used in frauds, generate numerous losses and even ruin the reputation of an organization. The fact is that organisations should seek to keep up with all these changes, not only to remain competitive, but also to protect their assets, investors and users.

IT governance is an excellent tool for this purpose, it is possible to glimpse its use in large organizations, but its processes could contribute a lot in smaller and/or non consolidated institutions.

Obviously, all this must be done in a cautious manner, since IT investments usually generate large financial outlays, and may not give the desired return. Through a well developed governance program, IT investments can be better directed, avoiding unnecessary expenses, as well as better results can be obtained by the sector.

It is fundamental the integration of the IT area, which usually acts in an isolated manner, with the other areas of the organizations so that their objectives are aligned to achieve the desired results, and for that, the participation and preparation of the managers is fundamental.

REFERENCES:

CARVALHO, Carlos A. da Costa. **What is IT Governance. IT Professionals**. Available at: <<https://www.profissionaisti.com.br/2009/03/o- who-governance-of-ti/>>. Accessed: 17 Aug. 2018.

CUNHA, M.S.; SOUZA NETO, J. **Comitês de governança de tecnologia da informação na administração pública federal brasileira: fatores críticos de sucesso.** Revista do Serviço Público, v. 65, n. 3, 2014. Available at: <https://revista.enap.gov.br/index.php/RSP/article/v iew/629/511>. Accessed: 28 Aug. 2018.

GASETA, E. R. **Fundamentos de Governança de TI. Rio de Janeiro:** Escola Superior de Redes, 2011. 102 p. Available at: <https://www.passeidireto.com/arquivo/16869959/f undamentos-de-governanca-de-ti>. Accessed: 27 Aug. 2018.

GOTARDO, R. **Governance in information technology.** Rio de Janeiro : SESES, 2015.

MIORANDO, R.F.; RIBEIRO, J.L.D. **Uma análise**

of IT governance in a postgraduate program. Product & Production, vol. 15 n. 1, pp. 64-75. Fev. 2014: UFRGS. Available at: <http://seer.ufrgs.br/ProdutoProducao/article/view/ 34567/28684>. Accessed: 27 Aug. 2018.

TEODORO, A. N.; PRZEYBILOVICZ, E;

CUNHA, M. A. **Governança de tecnologia da informação: uma investigação sobre a representação do conceito.** In: R. Adm., São Paulo, v.49, n.2, abr./maio/jun. 2014, p.307-321.

WEILL, P.; ROSS, J. W. **How effective is your IT governance?** CISR, Cambridge, v. 5, sloan wp n. 1B, 4 p., Mar. 2005. Available at: <https://cisr.mit.edu/blog/documents/2005_03_1B_ HowEffIsYrITGov.pdf>. Accessed: 27 Aug. 2018.

STAIR, R.M.; REYNOLDS, G.W. **Principles of Information Systems.** Translation of the 9. ed. norte-americana. São Paulo: Cengage Learning, 2012.

CHAPTER 4

BUSINESS INFORMATION SYSTEMS:
A COMPARISON BETWEEN SIG AND SAD

Abstract: *The purpose of this paper is to inform about two methods of Information Technology that help managers to make decisions in organizations: the Decision Support System and the Management Information System, as well as present their origins, applications and differences between them.*

Keywords: *System. Decision. Managers. Information.*

1. INTRODUCTION

Technological evolution has revolutionised organisations as a whole. As a way of making processes faster, more agile, precise and dynamic, companies are surrounded by technology in all parts of their processes, from robots that mechanise and replace human labour, to spreadsheets and systems that increasingly assist directions in the tactical and strategic field.

Systems are everywhere. Small businesses, large retail chains, companies in various fields use computers to deal with thousands of pieces of data. And, of course, this has reached the decision makers. Means such as the Decision Support System and the Management Information System help managers to make fewer mistakes and make their analysis faster, with greater agility to meet market needs.

Stair(1998), states that: "information systems is a series of interrelated elements or components that collect (input), manipulate and store (process), disseminate (output) data and information and provide a feedback mechanism".

While Gil (1999), defines that "information systems comprise a set of human, material, technological and financial resources aggregated according to a logical sequence for the processing of data and the corresponding translation into information".

2. TYPES OF BUSINESS INFORMATION SYSTEM

Due to the existence of different interests, specialties and levels in an organization, several types of systems are required, because no single system can meet all the needs of a company. As such, there are four types of business information systems, these being:

2.1 Transaction Processing Systems (TPS):

It is what monitors a company's sales, receipts, profit, expenses and material flow transactions.

2.2 Management Information Systems (MIS):

Assists in control, decision making and administration at management level. Provides reports of the company's performance to be able to forecast improvements in the future.

2.3 Decision Support Systems (DSS):

It is decision making in relation to unusual problems, such as impacts on production scheduling and delayed investment.

2.4 Executive Support Systems (ESS):

These are the "master" decision making, they are long term and need common sense and perception, as the solution is established beforehand.

However, only two (GIS AND SAD) were chosen to be further explored and compared.

3. DECISION SUPPORT SYSTEM

Junior et al. (2006) define a decision support system as being computer systems with the objective of providing support to corporate decision making processes, being composed of: user interface, database and models, supporting semi-structured and unstructured decisions, under the decision maker's control.

For Santos (2010) the decision support system encompasses a class of information systems or knowledge-based systems, i.e., it refers to a decision-making model that takes into account a large number of variables so that it is possible to make a decision on a particular issue.

However, there is a disagreement about the actual definition of DMS. Keen (1980) quoted by Santos (2010) says that there is no precise definition of DSS including all its aspects, but only the part of decision making. To complement, Power (1997) cited by Santos (2010) says that the term decision support system has become worn out due to its use to define various types of systems that support decision making, sometimes many systems are called DSS without at least being one.

3.1 Brief History

According to Santos (2010) the decision support system began to be discussed in the mid-60s and 70s, being studied more intensively in the 80s. For Bispo (1998) the SADs emerged to support managers in solving unstructured problems, but due to the high cost, the specific use and the difficulty in operating it, made it difficult to invest in the sector. In this period, the SAD was developed by the company itself or by third parties, not being able at that time to provide good support in decision making.

In the 1980s, the first database management systems (DBMS) appeared, bringing a significant improvement to the access of available data, formatting, consultation and reports in a more practical, quicker and cheaper way (BISPO, 1998).

According to The (1998) and Weldon (1998) cited by Bispo (1998) in the 90s the CASE tools and the fourth generation languages appeared, which promised to solve the problems of those who needed sudden information, being possible to perform queries and make reports in a faster and more practical way. However, these tools were not versatile enough to meet the needs of managers.

In the last decade, with the growth of companies and the increase in the volume of stored data, there was the need to expand the number of managers, raising the need for data analysis, better developing the technology around. Then, several decision support systems were developed to support companies in their decisions. Today, several technologies are being developed in other countries and are simultaneously being developed in Brazil (BISPO, 1998).

3.2 Architectures

According to Santos (2010) several authors identify in a different way the components of a DSS. The author cites Sprage and Carlson (1982), where they identify three fundamental components of a decision support system: Database Management System (DBMS), which is a set of software responsible for managing a database, are designed to manage a large amount of information and have as their main objective to provide a way to retrieve information from database that is both convenient and efficient.; Basic Modeling Management System (MBMS), a software system that may contain several tools, datamining or a collection of mathematical or analytical models that can be easily accessed by the user and the Dialog Generation and Management System (DGMS), DMS interface that allows the user to interact with the software system.

As well as its definition, Santos (2010) says that there is no fully accepted taxonomy for SAD. Háttenschwiller (1999) cited by Santos (2010) differentiates it into active, passive and cooperative. It also defines a passive DMS as a system that does not bring suggestion or solution, but rather assists in the decision-making process. Active DMS as bringing solutions and suggestions and the cooperative DMS acting as an advisor to complete and modify the suggestions in decision making.

3.3 Applications

DMS is mainly applied at the tactical level, where department managers use information from the strategic and operational level to draw up more concrete execution plans than those seen in management. It is mainly more useful in non-routine decisions, as it generates complex reports with a greater variety of data and statistics.

Among the unique problems in which it is usually applied, we can cite several situations taken at specific times, such as: testing a greater production of a product at a certain time of year, in order to observe market response; projecting a possible moment in which a company project was delayed and its impacts; price formulation; production planning; budget preparation; remuneration analysis and logistics problems.

Although more applied to the tactical level, SAD can be used at all levels, given the variety of its reports.

4. MANAGEMENT INFORMATION SYSTEM

The SIG - management information system supports the planning and control functions of an organization, providing safe and timely information for decision making.

According to Stair and Reynolds (2002, p. 18) a Management Information System (MIS) comprises an organised collection of people, procedures, software, databases and devices that provide routine information to managers and decision makers.

The concept of Oliveira (2004, p. 40) defines Management Information System (MIS) as being a process of transformation of data into information that is used in the decision-making structure of the company, also providing the administrative support to improve the expected results.

It is possible to note how efficient the implementation of an information system is in an organisation. Data is collected, processed and transformed into information. This contributes to all the sectors that receive this information and can be generated whenever necessary.

4.1 Brief History

Before the popularization of computers, the information systems in organizations were basically made by archiving information in large files. Even though this was a simple technique, it demanded a lot of work and effort to keep the information updated, besides not facilitating data analysis.

As of the 60's with the popularization of microcomputers for companies, it was already possible to generate pre-defined reports such as profit reports, balance sheets and sales report. They were trying to have them act in the role of decision support, although they were not yet capable.

In the 1970s, with the emergence of microprocessors, new high level languages also emerged, giving rise to data transmission over networks. With this new generation of high speed processors, new programmes with a high degree of interactivity with the user, internet and the like, further boosted the world of computing.

Due to the great evolution of strategic management and globalisation, the 90s brought with them the introduction of strategic information systems, competitive advantage became a much-discussed topic in the management context and software companies began to develop various tools.

4.2 Their Roles

The main focus of GIS is operational efficiency, assisting all departments within an organisation.

According to Stair and Reynolds (2002, p. 18) the focus of a MIS is primarily on operational efficiency. Marketing, production, finance and other functional areas receive support from management information systems and are linked through a common database.

The basic purpose of a GIS is to help the company achieve its goals by providing its managers with details about the organization's regular operations so that they can control organize and plan more effectively and with greater efficiency. (STAIR and REYNOLDS, 2002, p. 278).

4.3 Advantages and Disadvantages

As an advantage, the MIS helps to make routine decisions within the organisation, as it generates simple reports that summarise other more complex reports coming from other sectors of the company, such as reports from the accounting, marketing or purchasing sectors. Through them, it is possible to make decisions in a faster way for not so complex problems. This type of agility allows a good control and general monitoring of the company, besides being able to simulate future situations.

However, there are inherent disadvantages to this very simplicity. The lack of advanced statistics and more complex data jeopardises its usefulness in more difficult, non-routine decisions. In a sense, its potential use is limited, inflexible and dependent on information coming from other sectors, especially through Transaction Processing Systems.

Some other advantages are: improvement in productivity and services; improvement in the organisational structure by facilitating the flow of information;

reduction of bureaucratic labour.

There is some resistance to its implementation which is linked to the following aspects: mistrust of computers; misinformation about the social effects of automation and the consequent fear of the worker becoming obsolete; reduction of freedom, since administrators limit their plans to the formal structure; leadership based more on technical capacity than on formal authority; organisation of the systems to be only rational, without considering the role of emotions and other affective phenomena which intervene in the decision-making process.

4.4 Implementation of the GIS

Each organisation has its own priorities, both technical and political, that should be considered, the important thing is that the analysis is comprehensive, the focus well clarified and the best use made of the information and system. Two initial questions should be asked:

1. What are you getting at?
2. how to get there?

"A strategic plan describes where a system or programme is, where you want it to be, and how it will get there." Davis & Rhyason,1994.

The strategic planning cannot be confused with the technical project that defines in detail how the system will be (data, interface, applications), while the former does not bring the definition of details, but the direction goals of the whole development, being prior to the project.

By definition, the project has 3 phases to be followed, as can be seen in the table below:

Table 1: GIS Implementation Phases

PHASE 1 - Preparation	**PHASE 2 - Development**	**PHASE 3 - Continuation**
Feasibility Study	Staff and user training	Reassessment of the strategic systems plan
Technology Introduction	Data conversion and	Introduction of new

	modelling	projects
Analysis of opportunities, market and potential	Priority should be given to applications that provide improved services to customers	Administration of the system will be centralised
Deepen contacts with potential partners for the next phases of the project	Prototype development	Integration of all sectors, eliminating storage redundancies
Specification of applications, cost and benefits	Operationalisation of the solution	External partnership for development and commercialisation

Org. Beatriz Sousa, (2018).

There are some considerations that should be taken into account during the development for the good functioning of the system: no module of the project should be started before all the resources have been secured; the software should be of high quality and easy to handle; all the applications should have concrete results to be liable to be disseminated, with a maximum deadline of one year, at the end of which a report should be produced clearly indicating the objectives and benefits foreseen and those actually achieved during the period.

There is no well-defined recipe on how to implement the MIS in each organization, or if it will give a great return or success for the company, given its high cost and that it will depend not only on the implementation, but in the following years. The work must occur in partnership with the entire team, a budget and project review must be done constantly and especially, always keep the team motivated, since no result is obtained only by the system or by a single individual.

The cost varies according to the type of organization, its size and the number of users who will use the system. There are several costs involved besides the implantation, such as investment in infrastructure, user training, system customization, maintenance and even support (when charged). There are several modalities of sale and rent to acquire the license to use the system or even lifetime license, which would be the purchase itself. Finally, it is indicated that before choosing the software, should be tested as much as possible to choose the best and most appropriate to the place where it will be applied.

Given the cost of deployment and maintenance, which in most cases is greater than the profit generated, it is not feasible to commercialize the data, besides the fact that the information is the greatest asset of a company. However, it can be taken into consideration the sale of services and some knowledge, having pre-established the criteria for commercialization, the buyer carries with him the concern that a data is constantly updated, and an outdated data is a doubtful data.

4.5 Differences between GIS and SAD

According to Oliveira (2002), the Management Information System (MIS) is the process of transforming data into information that is utilized in the organization's decision structure, further providing the administrative support to optimize expected results. As for the Decision Support System (SAD), according to Stair (1998), it is an organized set of people, procedures, software, databases and devices used to support decision making that is specific to a problem, it goes beyond a traditional information system since it provides assistance in the solution of complex problems.

The main difference between them is defined by Binder (1994):

"It consists in the fact that SAD are characterised by flexibility and adaptability to change. These changes occur, not only in the problem itself, but also in the context in which it is inserted and in the way of facing it."

The table below summarises the differences in the various areas between the systems:

Table 2: Differences between SAD and GIS in their different scopes:

Scope	SAD	GIS
Development	Users trained by a specialist	System specialists
Objectives	- Analysis and Decision Support; -Doing the right thing (effectiveness)	-Information processing; - Getting it right (efficiency)
Users	Middle managers and	Mid-level managers

	analysts	
Application	Operational decision	Production control, sales projection, cost analysis More structured problems
Speed	Shorter development time, more flexible	Slower
Database	Special	From the company
Reports	Interactive on a computer screen	Produced periodically

Org. Beatriz Sousa, (2018).

5. METHODOLOGY

This work used bibliographical research to elucidate everything related to Decision Support Systems and Management Information Systems.

6. CONCLUDING REMARKS

Through this research, it was possible to note the importance of systems to assist managers in decision making, as well as the means for the different types of choices that managers need to make. Technology is part of the entire corporate environment and knowing what the best use for each of the tools is ideal to become a good manager in the information age. In the case of complex decisions, of difficult analysis and that need greater statistical immersion, one should look to SAD. While for routine issues, of broader vision and that concern more the day-to-day of the organization, the ideal is to opt for a GIS.

7. REFERENCES

BISPO, C. A. F. **Uma análise da nova geração de sistemas de apoio à decisão**. Universidade São Paulo. São Carlos, 1998.

JUNIOR, R. F. T.; FERNANDES, F.C.F.; PEREIRA, N.A. **Decision support systems for production scheduling in market foundries**. Gestão & Produção, v.13, n.2, 2006. Available at: <http://www.scielo.br/pdf/gp/v13n2/31168> Accessed on: 22 August 2018.

SANTOS, L. C. G. Dos. **The importance of information technology in decision making**. Universidade Candido Mendes, 2010. Available at: <http://www.avm.edu.br/docpdf/monografias_publicadas/C204769.pdf> Accessed on: 22 August 2018.

OLIVEIRA, Djalma de Pinho Rebouças de. **Sistemas de Informações Gerenciais.** 9º ed. São Paulo: Atlas 2004.

STAIR, Ralph M. and REYNOLDS George W. **Principles of Information Systems: Uma abordagem Gerencial**. 4º ed. São Paulo: LTC, 2002.

MARIN, Claudio Felício. **Sistema de apoio à decisão para área de vendas de uma loja agropecuária utilizando Data Warehouse**. 2003. 60 f., il. Completion of Course Work (Graduation in Computer Science) - Center of Exact and Natural Sciences, Regional University of Blumenau, Blumenau, 2003. Available at: <http://www.bc.furb.br/docs/MO/2002/266444_1_1.pdf>. Accessed on: 26 Aug. 2018.

BARBOSA, Geane et al. **Decision Support System SAD**. 2008. Available at: <http://www.administradores.com.br/artigos/tecnologia/sistema-de-apoio-a-decisao-sad/26378/>. Accessed on: 26 Aug. 2018.

FIGUEIREDO, Hamilton. GIS in Concessionaires. In: FERRARI JÚNIOR, Roberto. **Journey to GIS**. Curitiva: Sagres, 1997. p. 1-187. Available at: <http://www2.dc.ufscar.br/~ferrari/viagem/cap14.html>. Accessed on: 25 Aug. 2018.

SUPERSOFT, Team. **How much does it cost to implement an ERP system?** 2016. Available at: <https://www.supersoft.com.br/blog/artigos/quanto-custa-implantacao-de-um-sistema-erp-2/>. Accessed on: 25 Aug. 2018.

O'BRIEN, James; MARAKAS, George. **Administração de Sistemas de Informação**. 15. ed. [S.l.]: Amgh Editora, 2013.

MIX
Papier aus verantwortungsvollen Quellen
Paper from responsible sources
FSC® C105338

Printed by Books on Demand GmbH, Norderstedt / Germany